Handy Florida Genealogy Handbook

I0450656

Gary L. Morris

©2015 Gary L. Morris

ISBN-13: 978-1507762295

ISBN-10: 1507762291

Table of Contents

Notes

Genealogical Research in Florida

Florida has a long and eventful history making it an interesting and ideal state in which to conduct research. There are many historical and genealogical records available for Florida but you won't have to dig too much for them; we'll show you exactly where they are. To get you started in tracing your Florida ancestry, we'll introduce you to those records, and help you to understand:

1. What they are
2. Where to find them
3. How to use them

These records can be found both online and off, so we'll introduce you to online websites, indexes and databases, as well as brick-and-mortar repositories and other institutions that will help with your research in Florida. So that you will have a more comprehensive understanding of these records, we have provided a brief history of the "Sunshine State" to illustrate what type of records may have been generated during specific time periods. That information will assist you in pinpointing times and locations on which to focus the search for your Florida ancestors and their records.

A Brief History of Florida

Europeans, especially the French and Spanish began colonization of Florida at the beginning of the 16th century. The first permanent settlement was established at what is modern day St. Augustine in 1565. The French and Spanish battled back and forth for control of the area until the early 17th century when England set its sights on the area. The battles for control of Florida were bloody and vicious until the British finally gained control of the region in 1763 by giving up possession of Havana, Cuba.

British rule lasted a mere 20 years however, the Spanish winning control of Pensacola in 1781 during the War for Independence. The Spanish were awarded the entire area as part of the peace treaty that ended the American \revolutionary War. The Spanish attracted settlers to the area through land grants, and many Spanish, new Americans from the north, and escaped slaves flocked to the area. Spain finally ceded the region to the United States after several U.S. military expeditions to the area, a period which also saw the first of the Seminole Wars.

In 1821 Andrew Jackson journeyed to Florida to establish a territorial government for the United States, during which time many new settlers from surrounding southern states arriving in large numbers. Florida was granted territorial status in 1822, and Tallahassee was elected as the State Capital in 1824. The onset of white European settlers led to much tension between them and the Native American populations, a situation which led to the Second Seminole War which lasted from 1835-1842. After the loss of many lives and $20 million in expenses, war came to an end with many of the native Seminoles escaping to the Everglades where they established lives for themselves away from the whites.

Florida was awarded statehood in 1845 at which time the population was around 90,000 inhabitants. The first major issue that the new state was to face was slavery, the majority of the population being in favor. There was concern about the growing opposition to slavery in the north however, and the state finally voted to secede from the Union on January 10, 1861. Florida entered the civil War with the rest of the confederacy, though no major battles were fought there. Federal troops finally occupied Tallahassee on May 10, 1865, and the Reconstruction Era began. Florida was readmitted to the Union in 1868, though Federal troops remained in Tallahassee until 1786.

Important Genealogical Dates in Florida History

1565 – First permanent settlement established at St. Augustine
1763 – Ceded to Great Britain from France, divided into East and West Florida
1783 – East Florida ceded by Great Britain to Spain
1795 – United States takes control of West Florida above the 31st parallel
1814 – U.S. forces capture Pensacola
1817 – First Seminole War ends
1819 – Spanish Florida ceded to the United States
1822 – Organized as U.S. territory
1829 – Spanish Law replaced by Territorial Council
1835 – Second Seminole War begins, ends 1842
1838 – Constitution drafted
1845 – Statehood awarded
1855 – Third Seminole War ends
1861 – Cedes from Union
1868 – Readmitted to Union

Famous Battles Fought in Florida

Although only a few, these battle accounts can be very effective in uncovering the military records of your ancestor. They can tell you what regiments fought in which battles, and often include the names and ranks of many officers and enlisted men. Following are the most famous battles fought in Florida and links to useful information about them.

Battle of Pensacola – 1781: http://battleofpensacola.com/

The Seminole Wars – 1817-1818, 1835-1842, 1855-1858: http://www.seminolewars.us/history.html

The Battle of Olustee - 1864: http://www.battleofolustee.org/

Colonial Florida Genealogical Records

The Colonial era in Florida is a very important genealogical stepping-stone for researching your Florida ancestry. The Spanish were the first to colonize Florida, and many records of Florida citizens were generated by them. The majority of Florida records for the Spanish periods are held in the *Papeles de Cuba* section of the *Archivo General de Indias* in Seville, Spain. Copies of the vast majority of available records of interest have been made, and a good many have been published and can be found in the following repositories:

P. K. Yonge Library of Florida History at the University of Florida in Gainesville - the best collection of documentation covering the Spanish periods in Florida. Its collection includes the East Florida Papers, calendars of the John Batterson Stetson Collection, and *Papeles Procedentes de Cuba*.

P. K. Yonge Library of Florida History: http://web.uflib.ufl.edu/spec/pkyonge/brdrland.html.

The **St. Augustine Foundation Center for Historic Research** at Flagler College in St. Augustine holds well over 900 reels of primary documents on microfilm from Spanish and Spanish American archives, including a large library of secondary materials relating to Spanish Florida.

St. Augustine Foundation Center for Historic Research: http://www.flagler.edu/safoundation.html

St. Augustine Historical Society has a research library containing over 8,500 books, manuscripts, documents, and historical papers on Florida history.

St. Augustine Historical Society: http://www.staugustinehistoricalsociety.org/library.html.

Common Florida Genealogical Issues and Resources to Overcome Them

Boundary Changes: Boundary changes are a common obstacle when researching Florida ancestors. You could be searching for an ancestor's record in one county when in fact it is stored in a different one due to historical county boundary changes. The **Atlas of Historical County Boundaries** can help you to overcome that problem. It provides a chronological listing of every boundary change that has occurred in the history of Florida.

Atlas of Historical County Boundaries:
http://publications.newberry.org/ahcbp/documents/FL_Consolidated_Chronology.htm#Consolidated_Chronology

Name Changes: Surname changes, variations, and misspellings can complicate genealogical research. It is important to check all spelling variations. Soundex, a program that indexes names by sound, is a useful first step, but you can't rely on it completely as some name variations result in different Soundex codes. The surnames could be different, but the first name may be different too. You can also find records filed under initials, middle names, and nicknames as well, so you will need to **get creative with surname variations** and spellings in order to cover all the possibilities. For help with surname variations read our instructional article on **How to Use Soundex**.

get creative with surname variations:
http://obituarieshelp.org/blog/?p=634

How to Use Soundex: http://obituarieshelp.org/blog/?p=505

Florida Genealogical Organizations and Archives

Genealogical resources include not only records, but the organizations that house them, or can direct you to them. These institutions include: *Archives, Libraries, Genealogical Societies, Family History Centers, Universities, Churches, and Museums.*

Following are links to their websites, their physical addresses, and a summary of the records you can find there.

Archives

Florida State Archives and Library – Seminole War service records, Revolutionary Ware pension and bounty-land warrant applications, Mexican War muster rolls, Civil War service records, pension files, and muster rolls, Spanish-American War service records, WWI records, deeds, Tax rolls, marriage records, probate records, census records, cemetery records, burial records, county histories, historical maps and photographs, and more

R.A. Gray Building
500 South Bronough Street
Tallahassee, FL 32399-0250
Tel: 850-245-6700
Email: info@dos.myflorida.com

Florida State Archives and Library:
http://dlis.dos.state.fl.us/archives/genealogy.cfm

National Archives Southeast Region (Atlanta) – census indexes, passenger arrivals lists, Freedmen's records, pension files, naturalization records, land records, military records

5780 Jonesboro Road
Morrow, Georgia 30260
Tel: 770-968-2100
Fax: 770-968-2547

National Archives Southeast Region (Atlanta):
http://www.archives.gov/atlanta/

University of Florida – wide variety of genealogical and historical resources

Smathers Library Room 100
P.O. Box 117007
Gainesville, FL 32611
Telephone: 352-392-0319
Fax: 352-392-4788

University of Florida: http://www.uflib.ufl.edu/

FSU Libraries Special Collections and Archives - original primary source materials including unique manuscripts, historic maps, rare books, and historical photographs

Special Collections and Archives
Robert Manning Strozier Library
116 Honors Way
Tallahassee, FL 32306-2047
Tel: 850 644-3271

FSU Libraries Special Collections and Archives:
http://www.lib.fsu.edu/specialcollections

Florida Genealogical and Historical Societies

Genealogical and historical societies have access to extensive catalogues of genealogical data. They are also able to offer expert guidance for genealogical researchers. Many members are professional genealogists who are most willing to share their expertise in finding ancestors.

Florida Historical Society - an extensive collection, of maps, manuscripts, and photographic holdings

435 Brevard Ave.,
Cocoa ,FL 32922
Tel: 321-690-1971
Florida Historical Society: http://myfloridahistory.org/library

Florida State Genealogical Society – cemetery records, surname index, county histories

Florida State Genealogical Society
P.O. Box 940927
Maitland, FL 32794-0927
Tel: (407) 494-3747
Email: info@flsgs.org

Florida State Genealogical Society: http://flsgs.org/

Cuban Genealogy Club of Miami – cemetery records, census records, land records, civil registries, church records, historical newspapers, and more

5521 SW 163 Avenue
Southwest Ranches, FL 33331
Email: secretary@cubangenclub.org

Cuban Genealogy Club of Miami :
http://www.cubangenclub.org/cpage.php?pt=6

Tallahassee Genealogical Society – census records, family histories, immigration records, military records, periodicals

P.O. Box 4371
Tallahassee, FL 32315-4371
Email: tgspresident@gmail.com

Tallahassee Genealogical Society:
http://www.rootsweb.ancestry.com/~fltgs/?cj=1&netid=cj&o_xid=0
001231185&o_lid=0001231185&o_sch=Affiliate+External

Suwannee Valley Genealogy Society – voters list, land grant index, historical records

PO Box 967
Live Oak, FL 32064
Tel: 386-330-0110
Email: JinnieSVGS@windstream.net

Suwannee Valley Genealogy Society: http://www.svgsoc.org/

Florida Family History Centers

The Family History Centers run by the LDS Church offer free access to billions of genealogical records for free to the general public. They also provide classes on genealogy and one-on-one assistance to inexperienced family historians. Here you will find a **Complete Listing of Florida Family History Centers**.

Complete Listing of Florida Family History Centers:
https://familysearch.org/locations/centerlocator

Additional Florida Genealogical Resources

Florida Mailing Lists

Mailing lists are internet based facilities that use email to distribute a single message to all who subscribe to it. When information on a particular surname, new records, or any other important genealogy information related to the mailing list topic becomes available, the subscribers are alerted to it. Joining a mailing list is an excellent way to stay up to date on Florida genealogy research topics. Rootsweb have an extensive listing of **Florida Mailing Lists** on a variety of topics.

Florida Mailing Lists:
http://lists.rootsweb.ancestry.com/index/usa/FL/misc.html

Florida Message Boards

A message board is another internet based facility where people can post questions about a specific genealogy topic and have it answered by other genealogists. If you have questions about a surname, record type, or research topic, you can post your question and other researchers and genealogists will help you with the answer. Be sure to check back regularly, as the answers are not emailed to you. The Florida message boards at **Rootsweb** are completely free to use.

Rootsweb:
http://boards.rootsweb.com/localities.northam.usa.states/mb.ashx

<u>Florida Newspapers and Periodicals</u>

Many genealogy periodicals and historical newspapers contain reprinted copies of family genealogies, transcripts of family Bible records, information about local records and archives, census indexes, church records, queries, land records, obituaries, court records, cemetery records, and wills. The following sites have historical Florida newspapers and periodicals that you can search online or on-site.

Florida Digital Newspaper Library – historical, military, and ethical newspapers from Florida and the Caribbean

Florida Digital Newspaper Library: http://ufdc.ufl.edu/fdnl1

University of Central Florida Libraries – wide variety of Florida periodicals and magazines, especially valuable is their Historical Abstracts Index, which indexes thousands of journals, books, collections, and dissertations, related to world history events from 1450 to the present

University of Central Florida
P.O. Box 162666
Orlando, FL 32816-2666
Tel: 866-271-7589

University of Central Florida Libraries : http://guides.ucf.edu/content.php?pid=31986&sid=449389

Florida Online Historical Newspapers Index – index to historical newspapers available online dating from the late 19th century to present

Florida Online Historical Newspapers Index: https://sites.google.com/site/onlinenewspapersite/Home/usa/fl

The Online Books Page – links to historical books and periodicals available for viewing online, dating from mid-16th century

The Online Books Page: http://onlinebooks.library.upenn.edu

NewspaperArchive.com – largest online database of historical newspapers in the world.

NewspaperArchive.com: http://newspaperarchive.com/

Historical Florida Maps and Gazetteers

Maps are an integral part of genealogical research. They help us to locate landmarks, towns, cities, parishes, states, provinces, waterways and roads and streets. They also help us to determine when and where boundary changes might have taken place, and give us a visualization of the area we're researching in. For locating place names, a gazetteer is the best possible resource for any genealogist. Gazetteers are also sometimes called "place name dictionaries", and can help you to locate the area in which you need to conduct research. Below are links to the maps and gazetteers for research in Florida.

Peabody GNIS Service – Florida:
http://peabody.research.yale.edu/cgi-bin/Query.GNIS?ST=Florida&SU=1

Color Landform Atlas – Florida:
http://fermi.jhuapl.edu/states/fl_0.html

1985 U.S. Atlas link to: http://www.livgenmi.com/1895/FL/

Florida Hometown Locator: http://florida.hometownlocator.com/

Florida City Directories

.

City directories are similar to telephone directories in that they list the residents of a particular area. The difference though is what is important to genealogists, and that is they pre-date telephone directories. You can find an ancestor's information such as their street address, place of employment, occupation, or the name of their spouse. A one-stop-shop for finding city directories in Florida is the **Florida Online Historical Directories** which contains a listing of every available city and historical directory related to Florida. City directories can also be found in many local libraries.

Florida Online Historical Directories link to:
https://sites.google.com/site/onlinedirectorysite/Home/usa/fl

Jacksonville Public Library – Jacksonville city directories from 1876-1925

Main Library
303 N. Laura Street
Jacksonville, FL 32202
Tel: (904) 630-2665

Jacksonville Public Library:
http://jpl.coj.net/coll/florida/cdindex.html

Florida Historical Society – Various city directories from around the state

435 Brevard Ave.,
Cocoa ,FL 32922
Tel: 321-690-1971
Florida Historical Society: http://myfloridahistory.org/library

Florida Genealogical Records

<u>Birth, Death, Marriage and Divorce Records</u> – Also known as vital records, birth, death, and marriage certificates are the most basic, yet most important records attached to your ancestor. The reason for their importance is that they not only place your ancestor in a specific place at a definite time, but potentially connect the individual to other relatives. Below is a list of repositories and websites where you can find Florida vital records

Florida Bureau of Vital Statistics - birth records 1917-present, deaths records 2007 - present, marriage and divorces reports 1970 – present

Mailing address:

Bureau of Vital Statistics
Attn: Vital Records Section
P.O. Box 210
Jacksonville, FL 32231-0042
Tel: 904 359-6900
Email: VitalStats@doh.state.fl.us

Physical Address:

Bureau of Vital Statistics
1217 Pearl St.
Jacksonville, FL 32202

Florida Bureau of Vital Statistics:
http://www.floridahealth.gov/certificates-and-registries/certificates/index.html

Florida, Births and Christenings, 1880-1935 - index to birth, baptism and christening records from the state of Florida during the listed time period; some records may be even earlier

Florida, Births and Christenings, 1880-1935 -
https://familysearch.org/search/collection/1674799

Florida Marriages Database – Online Florida marriage records from 1822-1875

Florida Marriages Database: http://www.vitalsearch-ca.com/gen/fl/_vitals/flmarrim-go.htm

Florida, Marriages, 1830-1993 – Online index to Florida Marriages

Florida, Marriages, 1830-1993: https://familysearch.org/search/collection/1803936

Florida, Divorce Index, 1927-2001 – index to Florida divorces from the Office of Vital Records

Florida, Divorce Index, 1927-2001: https://familysearch.org/search/collection/1967745

Florida, Death Index, 1877-1998 - Index of deaths from the Florida Office of Vital Records

Florida, Death Index, 1877-1998: https://familysearch.org/search/collection/1946805

Census Reports

Census records are among the most important genealogical documents for placing your ancestor in a particular place at a specific time. Like BDM records, they can also lead you to other ancestors, particularly those who were living under the authority of the head of household.

Florida census records exist from 1850-1930 and many images and indexes can be viewed online. Following are the best places to find Florida census records.

Access Genealogy – Florida census records from 1850 indexed by individual county; includes Native and African American reports

Access Genealogy:
http://www.accessgenealogy.com/census/florida-census-records.htm

U.S National Archives – Federal census records on microfilm available from 1790 to 1940.

The National Archives and Records Administration
8601 Adelphi Road
College Park, MD 20740-6001

U.S National Archives: http://www.archives.gov/research/census/

Florida State Archives and Library – Complete Florida census collection

R.A. Gray Building
500 South Bronough Street
Tallahassee, FL 32399-0250
Tel: 850-245-6700
Email: info@dos.myflorida.com

Florida State Archives and Library:
http://dlis.dos.state.fl.us/archives/genealogy.cfm

National Archives Southeast Region (Atlanta) – Census indexes from 1790 onwards

5780 Jonesboro Road
Morrow, Georgia 30260
Tel: 770-968-2100
Fax: 770-968-2547

National Archives Southeast Region (Atlanta):
http://www.archives.gov/atlanta/

Florida Church Records

Church and synagogue records are a valuable resource, especially for baptisms, marriages, and burials that took place before 1900. You will need to at least have an idea of your ancestor's religious denomination, and in most cases you will have to visit a brick and mortar establishment to view them.

Most church records are kept by the individual church, although in some denominations, records are placed in a regional archive or maintained at the diocesan level. Local Historical Societies are sometimes the repository for the state's older church records. Below are links archives that maintain church records, as well as a few databases that can be viewed online.

The **Family History Library** contains many church records from a variety of denominations on microfilm.

Family History Library:
http://familysearch.org/learn/wiki/en/Family_History_Library

State Archives of Florida – wide variety of various denominational church records on microfilm

R.A. Gray Building
500 South Bronough Street
Tallahassee, FL 32399-0250
Tel: 850-245-6700
Email: info@dos.myflorida.com

State Archives of Florida:
http://dlis.dos.state.fl.us/barm/rediscovery/default.asp?IDCFile=/fsa/detailss.idc,SPECIFIC=2511,DATABASE=SERIES,

Cuban Genealogy Club of Miami – records from Cuban churches in Florida

5521 SW 163 Avenue
Southwest Ranches, FL 33331
Email: secretary@cubangenclub.org

Cuban Genealogy Club of Miami:
http://www.cubangenclub.org/cpage.php?pt=69

Church records Project at Rootsweb – online transcriptions of a variety of church records from around Florida

Church records Project at Rootsweb:
http://www.rootsweb.ancestry.com/usgenweb/churches/fl.html

Central Repositories for Denominational Records

Most of the records of individual denominations are kept in central repositories. Below is a list of the major congregational archives in Florida with links to their websites, physical addresses, and contact information.

Baptist

Florida Baptist Historical Society
5400 College Drive
Graceville, FL 32440
Tel: 800- 328-2660, ext. 480

Florida Baptist Historical Society:
http://www.floridabaptisthistory.org/

Methodist

Florida United Methodist Archives
Roux Library - Florida Southern College
111 Lake Hollingsworth Drive
P.O. Box 3767
Lakeland, FL 33801-5698
Tel: 863- 680-4164

Florida United Methodist Archives:
https://www.flsouthern.edu/library/

Roman Catholic

Archdiocese of Miami
9401 Biscayne Boulevard
Miami Shores, FL 33138
Tel: 305-757-6241
Fax: 305-754-1797

Archdiocese of Miami: http://www.miamiarch.org/

Diocese of Orlando
P.O. Box 1800
Orlando, Florida 32802-1800
Tel: 407-246-4800
Fax: 407-246-4942
Email: cbrinati@orlandodiocese.org

Diocese of Orlando: http://www.orlandodiocese.org/

Diocese of Pensacola-Tallahassee
11 North B St.
Pensacola, FL 32502
Tel: 850- 435-3500

Diocese of Pensacola-Tallahasseeo: http://www.ptdiocese.org/

Diocese of St. Augustine Archives
P.O. Box 3506
St. Augustine, FL 32085
Tel: 904- 823-8707 or 904- 806-2131

Diocese of St. Augustine Archives:
http://www.dosafl.com/NavLanding.asp?ID=190

Diocese of St. Petersburg
6363 9th Ave. N
St. Petersburg, FL 33710
Tel: 727- 344-1611

Diocese of St. Petersburg:
http://home.catholicweb.com/DOSParchive/

Diocese of Venice
1000 Pinebrook Road
Venice, FL 34285
Phone: (941) 484-9543

Diocese of Venice: http://dioceseofvenice.org/

Florida Military Records

More than 40 million Americans have participated in some time of war service since America was colonized. The chance of finding your ancestor amongst those records is exceptionally high. Military records can even reveal individuals who never actually served, such as those who registered for the two World Wars but were never called to duty.

Below are a number of links to websites and archives that contain Florida military records.

Florida State Archives and Library – Seminole War service records, Revolutionary Ware pension and bounty-land warrant applications, Mexican War muster rolls, Civil War service records, pension files, and muster rolls, Spanish-American War service records, WWI records

R.A. Gray Building
500 South Bronough Street
Tallahassee, FL 32399-0250
Tel: 850-245-6700
Email: info@dos.myflorida.com

Florida State Archives and Library:
http://dlis.dos.state.fl.us/archives/genealogy.cfm

U.S. National Archives – WWI Draft registration cards, casualties lists, WWI and WWII service records, Korean War records, Vietnam War records, Civil War and Spanish-American War records, and casualties lists.

U.S. National Archives:
http://www.archives.gov/research/military/veterans/online.html

US Department of Veterans Affairs Nationwide Gravesite Locator – includes information on veterans and their family members buried in veterans and military cemeteries having a government grave marker.

US Department of Veterans Affairs Nationwide Gravesite Locator: http://gravelocator.cem.va.gov/

United States Index to Indian Wars Pension Files, 1892-1926 – military pension records of soldiers who fought in the Indian Wars between 1817 and 1898

United States Index to Indian Wars Pension Files, 1892-1926: https://familysearch.org/search/collection/1979427

United States Mexican War Pension Index, 1887-1926 - index to Mexican War pension files for service between 1846 and 1848

United States Mexican War Pension Index, 1887-1926 : https://familysearch.org/search/collection/1979390

Civil War Soldiers Service Records - Service records for both Union and Confederate soldiers indexed by soldier's name, rank, and unit.

Civil War Soldier Service Records: http://go.fold3.com/civilwar_records/

Florida Cemetery Records

As convenient as it is to search cemetery records online, keep in mind that there are a few disadvantages over visiting a cemetery in person. They are:

- Tombstone information is not always accurately transcribed
- The arrangement of the graves in a cemetery can be crucial as family members are often buried next to each other or in the same grave. This arrangement is not always preserved in the alphabetical indexes that are found online.

With that information in mind, the following websites have databases that can be searched online for Florida Cemetery records.

Florida Tombstone Transcription Project - death and burial records

Florida Tombstone Transcription Project:
http://www.usgwtombstones.org/florida/florida.htm

African American Cemeteries Online – African American, slave, and Native American cemetery records

African American Cemeteries Online:
http://africanamericancemeteries.com/

Access Genealogy – huge database of Florida cemetery record transcriptions

Access Genealogy:
http://www.accessgenealogy.com/cemetery/florida.htm

Find a Grave – over 100 million grave records can be searched on this site. Search can be conducted by name, location, or cemetery name.

Find a Grave: http://www.findagrave.com/

Interment.net - A free online database containing approximately 4 million cemetery records from around the world.

Interment.net: http://www.interment.net/

Billion Graves – as the name implies, you can search a billion records including headstone photos, transcriptions, cemetery records, and grave locations.

Billion Graves:
http://billiongraves.com/pages/search/index.php#cemetery

Florida Obituaries

Obituaries can reveal a wealth about our ancestor and other relatives. You can search our **Florida Newspaper Obituaries Listings** from hundreds of Florida newspapers online for free.

Florida Newspaper Obituaries Listings:
http://obituarieshelp.org/florida_newspaper_obituaries.html

Florida Wills and Probate Records

The documents found in a probate packet may include a complete inventory of a person's estate, newspaper entries, witness testimony, a copy of a will, list of debtors and creditors, names of executors or trustees, names of heirs. They can not only tell you about the ancestor you're currently researching, but lead to other ancestors. Most of these records must be accessed at a county court or clerk's office, but some can be found online as well. You can obtain copies of the original probate records by writing to the county clerk.

Florida Department of State Division of Library and Information Services – Supreme Court records dating from the early 19th century

Florida Department of State Division of Library and Information Services:
http://www.floridamemory.com/collections/supremecourt/

MyFloridaCounty.com – searchable online database of Florida court and probate records

MyFloridaCounty.com:
https://www.myfloridacounty.com/ori/index.do

Florida Court Clerks and Comptrollers - list of Florida County clerks with addresses, contact numbers, and links to county websites containing information that can help obtain records, including costs.

Florida Court Clerks and Comptrollers:
http://www.flclerks.com/directory.html

The Family History Library maintains microfilmed copies of some Florida probate records which can be viewed at **Florida Family History Centers**. Records include:

1. Judges' administrations, 1847-1928
2. Local and foreign wills, 1847-1930
3. Probate packets, 1834-1944
4. Guardianships, 1886-1929
5. Register of estates, 1893-1926
6. Court Minutes, 1882-1928
7. General index to estates, 1834-1944

Florida Family History Centers :
http://familysearch.org/learn/wiki/en

Florida Immigration and Naturalization Records

The naturalization process generated many types of records, including petitions, declarations of intention, and oaths of allegiance. These records can provide family historians with information such as a person's birth date and place of birth, immigration year, marital status, spouse information, occupation, witnesses' names and addresses, and more.

Records of the Immigration and Naturalization Service, 1891-1957 - Passenger Lists of Vessels Arriving at Ports in Florida, 1890-1924, Passenger Lists of Vessels Arriving at Key West, FL, 1898-1945

Records of the Immigration and Naturalization Service, 1891-1957 : http://www.archives.gov/research/immigration/immigration-records-1891-1957.html

US National Archives – Immigration and Naturalization records for the entire United States

US National Archives: http://www.archives.gov/research/immigration/passenger-arrival.html

Family Search has the following indexes which can be vewed online for free:

Florida, Key West Passenger Lists, 1898-1945: https://familysearch.org/search/collection/1916042

Florida, Tampa, Passenger Lists, 1898-1945: https://familysearch.org/search/collection/1916082

United States Index to Passenger Arrivals, Atlantic and Gulf Ports, 1820-1874: https://familysearch.org/search/collection/1921756

Florida Native American Records

Florida Native American Heritage – wide variety of resources for tracing Native American Genealogy in Florida

Florida Native American Heritage: http://beyreuth.net/NatAmer/

Access Genealogy – Native American census records, tribal histories, and much more

Access Genealogy: http://www.accessgenealogy.com/native/

US National Archives - Microfilmed Records Pertaining to Enumeration of Seminole Indians in Florida, 1880-1940

US National Archives:
http://www.archives.gov/research/census/native-americans/seminole-enumeration.html

Bureau of Indian Affairs: http://www.bia.gov/

American Indians Records Repository - records dating from the 1700s including trust, education and other historic Indian Affairs records

American Indian Records Repository
Meritex Enterprises
17501 West 98th Street
Lenexa, KS 66219
Phone: 913-888-0601

American Indians Records Repository:
http://www.doi.gov/ost/records_mgmt/american-indian-records-repository.cfm

Missing Matriarchs – Resources for Researching Female Florida Ancestors

Looking for female ancestors requires an adjustment of how we view traditional records sources. A woman's identity was often under that of her husband, and often individual records for them can be difficult to locate. The following resources are effective in locating female ancestors in Florida where traditional records may not reveal them.

Marriage and Divorce Records

The earliest available marriage records date from 1822. State-wide registration didn't begin until 1927. Most marriage and divorce records for this period can be found at the Florida Department of Health in Jacksonville, but many county records can also be found on microfilm at the Florida State Archives in Tallahassee. They include the following:

1. Dade County marriages, 1840-1871 (film 1010085), Dade County marriage license applications, 1887-1892 (film 1870454 ff.), and marriage records, 1905-1911 (film 1010085) at the Dade County Records Center in Miami.
2. Escambia County marriage records, 1822-1927 (film 0941001 ff.) at the Escambia County Courthouse and the **Special Collections of the University of West Florida**, Pensacola.

Special Collections of the University of West Florida:
http://libguides.uwf.edu/universityarchives

Bibliographies

1. *Florida Pioneers and Their Descendants*, Anne Taylor Wood (Florida State Genealogical Society, 1992)
2. *Anglo-Americans in Spanish Archives: Lists of Anglo-American Settlers in the Spanish Colonies of America; A Finding Aid,* Lawrence H. Feldman (Genealogical Publishing Company, 1991)
3. *Women of Florida,* Lucy W. Blackman (Southern Historical Publishing, 1940)

Selected Resources for Florida Women's History

Broward County Women's History Coalition
1350 East Sunrise Boulevard
Suite 114
Fort Lauderdale, FL 33304

Community Coalition for Women's History
352 NW 5th St.
Miami, FL 33128-1615

Common Florida Surnames

The following surnames are among the most common in Florida and are also being currently researched by other genealogists. If you find your surname here, there is a chance that some research has already been performed on your ancestor.

Abney, Akins, Alexander, Allen, Anderson, Arnold, Baker, Barron, Barrow, Bennett, Berg, Beville, Bird, Black, Bradham, Branch, Brett, Bridges, Brown, Bryant, Caruthers, Cassidy, Cavous, Chandler, Cocowitch, Condrey, Cook, Crawford, Crenshaw, Crews, Curry, Dixon, Dorminy, Douglas, Douglass, Dozier, Drawdy, Driggers, Durrance, Dyess, Dykes, Dickson, Eldridge, Ellis, Eubank, Eubank, Fender, Fitzgerald, Fort, Fussell, Gandie, Garner, Gant, Giddeons, Gideon, Grant, Geiger, Godfrey, Godwin, Gough, Gray, Green, Griffin, Groff, Gunn, Hadsade, Hall, Hamilton, Harrell, Harris, Hawkins, Hays, Hodge, Hope, Hudson, Hunt, Jernigan, Jones, Knight, Lane, Lawrence, Lee, Long, Lovett, Leitner, Mainor, Manor, Marlow, Martin, Matteson, Maynard, McClendon, McDermitt, McMullin, McPherson, Mercer, Merritt, Merline, Miller, Mixon, Mobley, Moore, Mott, Murrhee, Nesbitt, Norman, O'Berry, Olive, Orr, Paulk, Pemberton, Perry, Phelps, Pinner, Pelton, Powell, Prevatt, Rackley, Ramage, Revels, Richerson, Roach, Robertson, Shaw, Simmons, Sims, Smith, Sparkman, St. Clair, Stafford, Stewart, Stivender, Stokes, Sutton, Tate, Thompson, Tiddwell, Tucker, Turnage, Ussey, Varn, Vining, Voyles, Wade, Warren, Watson, Watson, Whidden, Whidden, Whiddon, Wicker, Wightman, Williams, Wilson, Wing, Wolf (Woolf), Woodard, Wright,Yates

About the Author

Gary L. Morris worked from 2009 to 2014 as a professional researcher for a major player in the genealogy field. After tracing his family lineage back to 1683, he found that genealogy could be an expensive undertaking. As such, has decided to publish these helpful guides to share the valuable free information he has discovered during his career to help others trace their family lineages as inexpensively as possible. An avid genealogist himself, he hopes you will find this guide factual, thorough, helpful, and most of all, effective in helping you to find your family members.

Notes

Notes

www.ingramcontent.com/pod-product-compliance
Lightning Source LLC
Chambersburg PA
CBHW061927280526
45787CB00004B/1507